What About the Other 90%?

A Biblical Guide to Financial Wisdom for
Immigrants

By Valencia J. Maponya

What About the Other 90%?

A Biblical Guide to Financial Wisdom for Immigrants

ISBN: 979-8-218-78731-8

Published by Roehampton Products, LLC

Printed in the United States of America

First Edition: 2025

Dedication

This book is dedicated to my beloved
son, Makobe C. Maponya, who gives
me reason and purpose.

Table of Contents

Chapter 1

Introduction –
More Than a Tithe

Imagine stepping through the doors of an international arrivals hall—your suitcase heavy, your pocket cradling the last of your savings or borrowed money, and your heart set on building a new life. You carry a quiet assurance: *"I can do all things through Christ who strengthens me"* (Philippians 4:13).

For many immigrants, this moment marks more than just a change of location—it begins a journey of faith, resilience, and stewardship. In this new land, every dollar earned, and every decision made carries the weight of responsibility: to provide for family, to honor God through wise management, and to build a foundation strong enough to bless future generations.

Whether you are a first-generation immigrant or part of the second, or third generation continuing the story, you have arrived—ready not only to survive but to understand the principles that lead to thriving. This is where faith meets finances, where purpose meets planning, and where community becomes the circle that sustains us all.

So now you have received your first paycheck—what's next? Many Christians understand the importance of giving 10%—the tithe—but what about the other 90%?

This book is a call to wise stewardship of every dollar God entrusts to us. Especially for immigrants navigating a new economic system, financial literacy grounded in biblical truth can make the difference between surviving and thriving. Psalm 24:1 sets the tone: *"The earth is the Lord's, and everything in it."* This verse is not merely theological—it is deeply practical. It reminds us that every dollar, every asset, and every opportunity belong to God. Our job, then, is to manage it faithfully.

For many immigrants, particularly from Caribbean and African nations, the concept of tithing is familiar. In fact, giving to one's church or community, even in times of lack, is often deeply rooted in their upbringing. However, there is often less emphasis on what to do with the remaining 90%—how to save, invest, budget, and protect family members through life insurance or retirement planning. This book addresses that gap.

In many Caribbean households, financial wisdom is taught through lived experience—children watching parents stretch income creatively. Still, systemic knowledge of banking, insurance, and investing is often limited. In African contexts, community support structures, extended families, and informal savings groups (like susu or stokvels) dominate financial practices. These can foster generosity and solidarity, but also leave individuals unprepared for navigating formal financial systems in the U.S.

Upon immigrating, many face a confusing world of credit scores, tax filings, and financial products that seem more like burdens than blessings. Without guidance, it's easy to make decisions based on survival, not stewardship. Yet God calls us to manage resources with intention and wisdom.

> *Survival decisions may keep you afloat.*
> *Stewardship decisions build legacy!*

Next Chapter Preview: Biblical Principles of Stewardship

This chapter introduces our foundational truth: stewardship is not about how much you have—it's about how faithfully you manage what you've been given. This book is your companion as you journey through budgeting, saving, giving, and growing— according to God's Word.

*Key Verse: Psalm 24:1 - "The earth is the Lord's, and everything in it."

NOTES

Chapter 2

Biblical Principles of Stewardship

Biblical stewardship is the understanding that we do not own anything—God owns it all. Our role is to wisely manage His resources, with integrity and obedience. The Bible is filled with principles to guide us in this responsibility.

1. God Owns Everything

Haggai 2:8 says, *"The silver is mine and the gold is mine,"* declares the Lord Almighty. From the money in our wallets to the homes we live in, everything we possess ultimately belongs to God. This truth should shape how we view spending, saving, and giving.

2. We Are Stewards, Not Owners

In Matthew 25:14–30, Jesus shares the Parable of the Talents. The master entrusts his servants with wealth while he is away, expecting them to manage it wisely. One servant hides the money, another invests it. The lesson is clear: God expects us to multiply and wisely use what He gives us—not just preserve it. Stewardship includes strategic planning, intentional saving and investing, and generous giving.

3. Avoid Debt

Romans 13:8 says, *"Let no debt remain outstanding, except the continuing debt to love one another."* Debt can become a form of bondage, limiting our freedom to follow God's call and provide for our families. While some forms of debt (like a mortgage) may be necessary, living within our means and paying off what we owe should be a priority.

> *Debt is a tool, but it can also be a trap. Freedom is found in living within your means!*

4. Plan Diligently

Proverbs 21:5 says, *"The plans of the diligent lead to profit as surely as haste leads to poverty."* Faithful stewardship requires us to be intentional. Planning a monthly budget, saving for future needs, and preparing for emergencies are all biblical practices.

5. Give Generously

2 Corinthians 9:7 teaches, *"Each of you should give what you have decided in your heart to give...for God loves a cheerful giver."* Giving is not about obligation—

it's about worship. When we give with joy, we reflect God's generosity to the world around us. Giving extends beyond tithing—it can include helping family, donating to missions, or supporting someone in crisis.

Stewardship as Worship

Ultimately, stewardship is an act of worship. How we handle money reflects our trust in God and our commitment to His kingdom. Every financial decision can be an opportunity to honor Him.

Reflection Questions
- What did your family teach you about money?
- How do your beliefs align with scripture?
- What stewardship habits do you want to adopt?

Take time to reflect honestly. Your past does not define your future. By applying biblical principles, you can build new habits that honor God and bless generations to come.

Next Chapter Preview:
Understanding the Economic Landscape

NOTES

Chapter 3

Understanding the Economic Landscape

Migrants from the Caribbean, Africa, Latin America, and parts of Asia often transition from economies that function very differently than the U.S. economy. Understanding these contrasts is essential to developing a wise and biblically grounded financial life in the U.S.

U.S. Economic Structure

- Capitalist system driven by private ownership, competitive markets, and innovation
- Heavy reliance on credit and digital banking
- Consumer-driven spending with sophisticated financial infrastructure
- Strong institutional regulation (e.g., Federal Deposit Insurance Corporation - FDIC, Federal Reserve)
- Safety nets include Social Security, Medicare, and unemployment benefits

Developing Economy Structures (Caribbean, Africa, Latin America, Asia)

- More informal markets, with many transactions conducted in cash
- Limited access to formal credit, insurance, or banking systems
- High reliance on family networks and community mutual aid
- Financial instability due to political risk, inflation, or currency fluctuation
- Often high remittance inflow from diaspora abroad

Key Differences

Category	United States	Developing Regions
Banking	Widespread access, digital tools	Limited reach, especially in rural areas
Credit Systems	Strong credit bureaus, lending options	Often high-interest microloans or cash-based
Financial Literacy	Promoted via institutions and schools	Often learned informally from family
Entre-preneurship	Institutional support, access to capital	Driven by necessity, with fewer protections
Investment Options	Diverse: stocks, mutual funds, retirement	Few long-term vehicles; real estate common

Informal Economy Role	Small	Major source of employment
Safety Nets	Government-sponsored (SSI, SNAP, etc.)	Largely family or church/ community based

Why This Matters for Immigrants

For immigrants, the why is answered by recognizing that financial literacy is not just a useful skill—it is a lifeline. Learning how to navigate the U.S. financial system equips individuals to make wise decisions about credit, banking, housing, insurance, and investing. Without this knowledge, it is easy to fall into costly traps, from predatory loans to burdensome debt. With it, however, immigrants can shift from a survival mindset to one of intentional stewardship. Financial literacy empowers families to plan, save, and give in ways that align with their values and faith. Proverbs 4:7 reminds us, *"The beginning of wisdom is this: Get wisdom. Though it cost all you have, get understanding."* Building financial understanding allows immigrants to strengthen their households today while laying a firm foundation for the generations that follow.

Understanding these differences equips you to:

- Adapt wisely to a system where credit and documentation matter
- Utilize U.S.-based tools like savings accounts, credit scores, and insurance
- Avoid predatory financial schemes
- Continue supporting family abroad while building your own legacy

Personal Story

When I arrived to the USA, I knew that I needed to build my credit and went to a major bank in Maplewood, New Jersey to open a secured credit card with $200. Fast forward, for some reason, I was helped by the Bank's Manager, and I remember her saying to me, let me tell you something about credit. She said, *"never exceed 29% of your credit limit especially on one card."* and went on to giving me a quick credit literacy class in those few moments. That interaction prompted my curiosity to understand that I should take personal note to differences in the economic structures.

Biblical Lens

Whether in the U.S. or abroad, God calls us to live wisely (Proverbs 4:7), avoid debt (Romans 13:8), and use money to care for others (Galatians 6:10). With understanding comes the power to steward well.

Income Generation

Expectations versus reality of the new life for many immigrants is one of the most difficult adjustments. When starting over on their journey, degrees, licenses, and work experience from abroad often do not transfer easily in the United States, leaving many highly skilled individuals working entry-level jobs just to survive. This reality can feel discouraging, but it also presents an opportunity to reimagine income generation. Note that the term income generation is intentionally used because the means for financial success may not reside in a profession as is known from 'back-home'. As such, some immigrants turn to entrepreneurship, side hustles, or retraining programs that open doors to new fields. Others choose to build slowly in their careers while supplementing income through gig work or small businesses. Above all, understand this: income generation is key to navigating the economic landscape of your new land. Nevertheless, no matter the path, Scripture reminds us: *"Whatever you do, work at it with all your heart, as working for the Lord, not for human masters"* (Colossians 3:23). Faithful diligence, even in humble beginnings, not only provides for today but can also lay the foundation for greater stability and opportunities tomorrow.

Navigating Taxes in the U.S.

For many immigrants, nothing feels more intimidating than the U.S. tax system. Forms filled with unfamiliar terms, deadlines that come quickly each year, and the fear of making mistakes can create anxiety. Yet, taxes are a reality of life in America, and learning to navigate them with wisdom is part of good stewardship.

Romans 13:6–7 reminds us: *"This is also why you pay taxes, for the authorities are God's servants, who give their full time to governing. Give to everyone what you owe them: If you owe taxes, pay taxes."* Paying taxes is not just a civic duty but also a spiritual one — an act of obedience and integrity that allows us to live peacefully and honorably in the land God has placed us.

Understanding and managing your taxes well help protect you from penalties, debt, and unnecessary stress. Further, understanding how taxes fit into the economic landscape will open doors to financial milestones, such as buying a home, applying for loans, or starting a business.

Key Elements of the U.S. Tax System

1. Social Security Number (SSN) or ITIN

- To file taxes, you need either a Social Security Number (SSN) or an Individual Taxpayer Identification Number (ITIN).
- An ITIN is available to immigrants who are not eligible for an SSN but still need to file taxes.

2. Income Reporting

- The U.S. requires you to report all forms of income: wages, self-employment, freelance work, and even certain income from abroad.
- Employers usually provide a W-2 form at year-end, while contractors receive a 1099.

3. Deductions and Credits

- Deductions lower your taxable income; credits reduce the taxes you owe.
- Common credits include the Child Tax Credit and the Earned Income Credit, which can provide significant refunds for working families.

4. Filing Deadline

- Tax returns are typically due by April 15 each year. Extensions are possible, but penalties may apply if you owe money and do not file.

5. State and Local Taxes

- In addition to federal taxes, many states and even some cities require separate filings. Each jurisdiction has different rules.

Common Mistakes to Avoid

- Not filing at all because of fear or confusion — even if you are undocumented, filing with an ITIN shows responsibility.

- Paying unnecessary fees to unscrupulous "tax preparers" who target immigrants. Always use trusted, certified tax help.

- Ignoring foreign income — certain types must be reported, even if small.

- Missing out on credits — many families leave money on the table simply because they do not know what they qualify for.

Wise Steps for Stewardship

- Keep records of income, receipts, and expenses throughout the year.

- Seek out free or low-cost help: programs like VITA (Volunteer Income Tax Assistance) provide trained volunteers who help immigrants file taxes accurately.

- Learn the basics of your own tax return. Even if you use a preparer, understanding what's on the forms empowers you to ask questions and avoid mistakes.

Pray for wisdom and remember that attending to your taxes reflects honesty before God and man. Taxes may feel like a burden, but when seen through the lens of Scripture, they become an opportunity to practice integrity and reflect God's order in our daily lives.

> Give to everyone what you owe them: If you owe taxes, pay taxes." – Romans 13:7

Worksheet: Economic Context Comparison – note your experience

Category	My Home Country Experience	My U.S. Experience
Banking		
Credit Use		
Support Systems		
Remittance Practices		
Saving and investing		
Taxes		

Reflection Questions

- What surprised you most about the U.S. system?
- What wisdom from your home culture is worth preserving?
- Since coming to the U.S., what has been the hardest part of learning the financial system?
- What steps have you already taken to increase your financial understanding?
- What new financial tools can help you walk in biblical stewardship here?

Next Chapter Preview: Creating a Kingdom Budget

We'll take a deep dive into how to manage income in a way that reflects God's priorities—covering everything from tithing to saving and daily spending.

NOTES

Chapter 4

Creating a Kingdom Budget

Creating a budget is a practical and spiritual step toward faithful stewardship. A Kingdom budget doesn't just focus on surviving the month—it reflects your values, goals, and commitment to honoring God with every dollar.

Step-by-Step Budgeting Guide

1. Track Your Income

- Identify all sources: wages, side hustles, benefits, etc.
- Make it monthly for consistency.

2. Give First

- Prioritize your tithe (10% or more if you're led).
- Giving should be intentional, not an afterthought (Proverbs 3:9).

3. Save Second

- Aim for at least 10% into savings.
- Build an emergency fund and long-term savings.

4. List Monthly Expenses

- Separate needs (rent, food, utilities) from wants (subscriptions, dining out).
- Allocate based on priorities.

5. Adjust & Review

- Budgets are living tools. Review them monthly.
- Involve your spouse or accountability partner.

Budgeting in Different Cultural Contexts

- **African & Caribbean traditions:** Many grow up using informal methods like cash envelopes or community savings (susu, partner).

- **Latin American families:** High emphasis on sending remittances home, often leaving little for personal savings.

- **In the U.S.:** Digital tools (apps, spreadsheets) can enhance these practices.

Use what's familiar—then build on it with better structure and biblical guidance.

Biblical Anchor:
"The plans of the diligent lead surely to abundance" – Proverbs 21:5

Worksheet: Monthly Budget Template

Category	Amount Budgeted	Amount Spent	Notes
Income			
Tithe & giving			
Savings			Emergency, Retirement
Housing (Rent/ Mortgage)			
Utilities			
Food & Groceries			
Transportation			Gas, Bus, Repairs
Health & Insurance			
Remittances			
Personal/Other			Entertainment, Phone, etc.
TOTALS			

Envelope System Tracker

Envelope Name	Budgeted Amount	Remaining Balance	Notes
Groceries			
Gas/Transport			
Giving			
Emergency Fund			

Use labeled envelopes or digital wallets to control spending in each category.

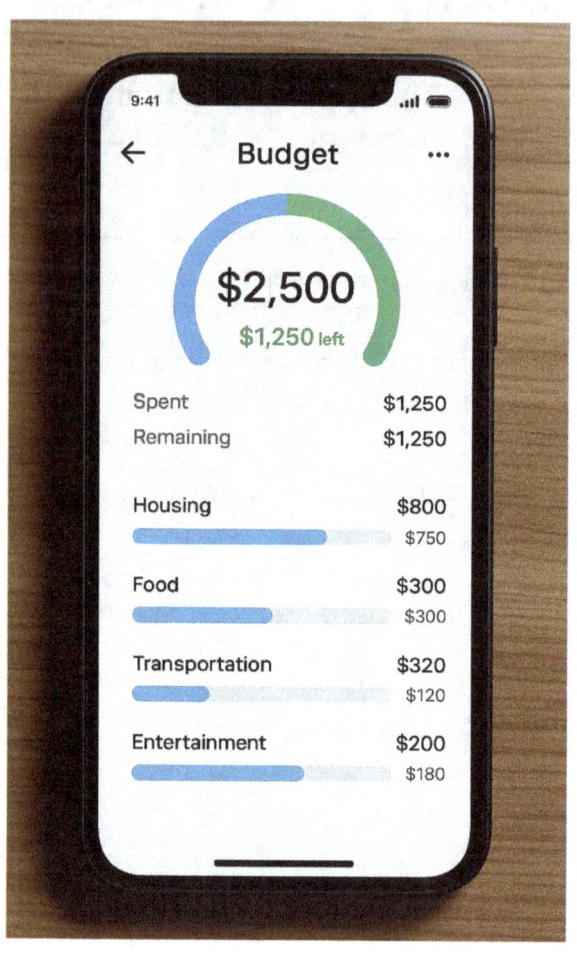

Reflection Questions

- What does your current budget say about your values?
- Does it reflect trust in God, generosity, and wisdom?

You are managing God's resources to bless your life and others.

Budgeting isn't about restriction – it's about vision!

3 Quick Wins to Start Budgeting Today

1. Track every expense for 7 days.
2. Cut one non-essential subscription.
3. Automate $25/month into savings.

Next Chapter Preview: The Role of Life Insurance

We'll look at how protecting your family through insurance can be a spiritual act of care, planning, and provision.

NOTES

Chapter 5

The Role of Life Insurance

Life insurance is one of the most overlooked but vital tools in a family's financial foundation. As immigrants, the challenge of supporting loved ones both here and abroad is complex. But one thing is clear: protecting your family from financial hardship after your death is both an act of love and stewardship.

Why Life Insurance Matters

Proverbs 13:22 reminds us, *"A good person leaves an inheritance for their children's children."* Life insurance is one way to ensure your family is not burdened with debt or loss of income after you're gone.

Whether you're single, married, or have children, life insurance can:

- Cover funeral and burial costs
- Pay off debts (credit cards, car loans, mortgage)
- Replace lost income for your family
- Cover children's education
- Prevent family back home from shouldering your

expenses

> *Life insurance = an inheritance of dignity, not debt!*

Types of Life Insurance

1. Term Life Insurance

- Provides coverage for a set period (e.g., 10, 20, 30 years)
- Lower cost, fixed premiums
- No cash value—only pays a death benefit
- Ideal for most working families

2. Whole Life Insurance

- Lifetime coverage
- Builds cash value over time
- Higher premiums
- Can be borrowed against but is more complex

3. Group Life Insurance

- Usually offered by employers, often free or at low cost
- Can be identified through credit unions, affiliation groups
- Limited amount (1-2x salary)
- Great as a supplement
- Strongly consider if you have pre-existing conditions

Get Insured Early

The younger and healthier you are, the cheaper your premiums will be. Waiting until later or after a health issue can make it harder or more expensive to qualify.

Trust-Based vs. Policy-Based Caregiving

In many cultures, caregiving is assumed to be handled by relatives. This trust-based system depends on others' goodwill. But in a new country, with increasing costs and individual responsibilities, policy-based caregiving—such as life insurance—ensures there's a plan and provision in place.

✓ **Checklist: Must-Have Protection**

- ☐ Health Insurance
- ☐ Life Insurance
- ☐ Auto/Renters Insurance
- ☐ Disability Insurance

Protect your family before you invest.

Worksheet: Life Insurance Needs Calculator

Financial Need Category	Estimated Amount (USD)
Funeral/Burial Costs	
Outstanding Debts (credit, car)	
Mortgage or Rent (years x cost)	
Children's Education	
Monthly Income Replacement (x years)	
Total Needed Coverage	

Reflection Questions

- Who depends on you financially?
- How would they manage without your income?
- Are you trusting goodwill alone or planning proactively?
- What are your monthly expenses?
- How many years would your family need support?

Next Chapter Preview: Preparing for Retirement

We'll explore how long-term planning is not just for the wealthy, but for every faithful steward—regardless of income or background.

NOTES

Chapter 6

Planning for Retirement

Planning for retirement is an act of both faith and wisdom. It reflects our understanding of seasons in life and our commitment to stewarding resources beyond today. For many immigrants, especially those from Caribbean, African, Latin American, and Asian backgrounds, retirement planning looks vastly different in the U.S. than it does in their countries of origin.

Retirement in the U.S. vs. Informal Support Systems

In many parts of the world, there's no pension or savings account waiting at age 65. Instead, older adults rely on their children, extended family, or community. This cultural value of interdependence is beautiful, but in the U.S., it's often not sustainable. Children may be navigating their own financial responsibilities, and the cost of living can make multigenerational support difficult.

By contrast, the U.S. system offers structured, regulated ways to save for retirement. These methods come with significant tax advantages and, when started early, can grow into meaningful retirement income.

Key U.S. Retirement Vehicles

1. 401(k)

- Offered by employers
- Contributions deducted from paycheck before taxes
- Many employers offer matching contributions (e.g., 5% up to 6%)
- Withdrawals allowed after age 59½ (taxed as income)

2. Traditional IRA (Individual Retirement Account)

- Contribute up to the maximum yearly limit set by the Internal Revenue Service -IRS; visit irs.gov for annual limit usually communicated in October for the upcoming year
- Tax-deferred growth
- Contributions may be tax-deductible

3. Roth IRA

- Contributions made with after-tax dollars with yearly limit set by the IRS
- Qualified withdrawals (after age 59½) are tax-free

- Great for lower-income earners or younger savers

4. Social Security

- Public benefit based on your work history in the U.S.
- Provides monthly income beginning as early as age 62

Why You Should Start Now

- Time allows your money to grow through **compound interest.**
- The earlier you start, the more you benefit—even if it's a small amount.
- Delaying retirement planning means you may have to work longer or rely on others.

Biblical Insight

"Go to the ant, you sluggard; consider its ways and be wise! It has no commander, yet it stores its provisions in summer and gathers its food at harvest." – Proverbs 6:6-8

Small, steady savings today secures tomorrow!

Planning for the future is wise and biblical. Just as Joseph stored up grain in Egypt during seven good years (Genesis 41), we are called to prepare for lean seasons, including old age.

Common Myths/Misconceptions

- *"God will provide."* Yes, but He calls us to act in wisdom and diligence.

- *"My children will take care of me."* They might— but shouldering that responsibility alone could be a heavy burden.

- *"It's too late for me to start."* Even in your 40s, 50s, or beyond, saving something is better than nothing.

Worksheet: Annual Retirement Goals Planner

Goal Category	Target Amount	Current Saved	Gap	Notes
Emergency Fund (3–6 months)				
Retirement Savings Target				15% of income suggested
Employer Match Utilized?	Yes/No			Confirm with HR
Estimated Monthly Retirement Income Needed				Based on current expenses

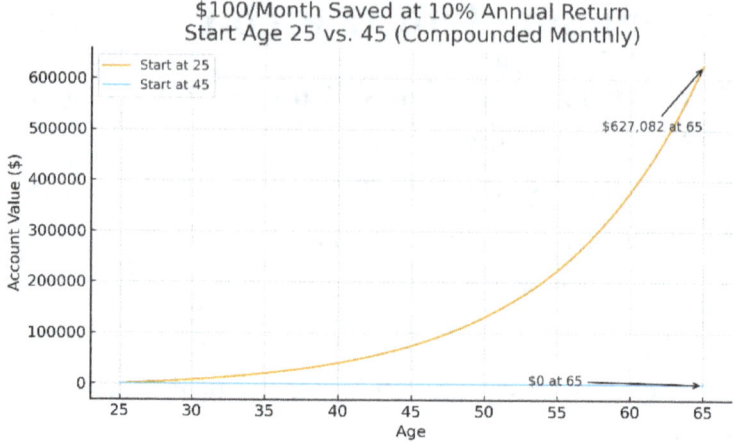

Figure 1: Growth comparison for retirement with $100 per month starting at age 25 vs. 45

Reflection Questions

- Have you considered how you want to live in retirement?

- What steps can you take today to make that vision possible?

- Are you missing out on any employer retirement benefits?

Encouragement God doesn't promise ease, but He does promise provision. When you plan with God's wisdom, you lay a foundation not only for your future, but also to bless generations after you.

Next Chapter Preview: Investing with Integrity

Learn how to multiply your resources through ethical investing while keeping your heart fixed on the Giver—not just the gift.

NOTES

Chapter 7

Investing with Integrity

Investing is about more than growing your money—it's about multiplying what God has entrusted to you in a wise and ethical way. For many immigrants, investing may seem like a luxury, or even a mystery, especially if it was not common in their country of origin. But understanding the basics—and applying biblical wisdom—can turn investing into an act of faithful stewardship.

What Is Investing?

Investing is putting your money to work so it can grow over time. This can take many forms, including:

- Buying shares of companies (stocks)
- Lending money to companies or governments (bonds)
- Owning a share of many companies (mutual funds or index funds)
- Buying real estate or property

Real-World Examples

1. Stocks

- A stock or share is buying ownership into a company

- Examples of companies that sell their stock are Amazon (AMZN), Apple (AAPL), Microsoft (MSFT)

2. Low-Cost Index Funds

- An index fund is a basket of stocks that mirrors a segment of the market, like the S&P 500.

- They're low-fee, passive investments great for beginners.

- Many immigrant families have built wealth over time by consistently contributing to these funds, often through retirement accounts.

- Examples include symbols VOO, VUG, SPY

3. Homeownership

- Many immigrant families prioritize buying a home. This can be both a personal milestone and a long-term investment.

Biblical Cautions: Avoid Greedy Speculation

Proverbs 13:11 warns, *"Dishonest money dwindles away, but whoever gathers money little by little makes it grow."* The Bible doesn't condemn investing—but it cautions against gambling, get-rich-quick schemes, and hoarding. True investing is about long-term thinking, not chasing fast profits.

> *Avoid gambling with God's resources. Grow it over time!*

Principles of Kingdom-Minded Investing

- **Integrity:** Avoid shady or deceptive schemes (Proverbs 10:9)

- **Patience:** Invest over time, not in hype

- **Purpose:** Invest with a plan to bless others and prepare for your future

- **Prayer:** Seek God's guidance, not just financial gain

Common Investment Types

Investment Type	Risk Level	Growth Potential	Notes
Savings Account	Low	Very Low	Best for emergencies
Bonds	Low-Med	Moderate	Safer than stocks, lower return
Index Funds	Med	High (long term)	Low fees, diversified
Individual Stocks	High	High	Risky—requires research

Real Estate	Med	High	Good for cash flow and appreciation

Worksheet: Investment Risk Profile

Question	Response
How many years until you need the money?	Short / Medium / Long
How do you feel about short-term losses?	Very Uncomfortable / Neutral / OK
What is your primary goal?	Safety / Growth / Income
How much can you afford to lose without panic?	None / A little / Some

Basic Diversification

(will vary and is determined according to the investor's circumstances, such as age)

Suggested Portfolio Allocation

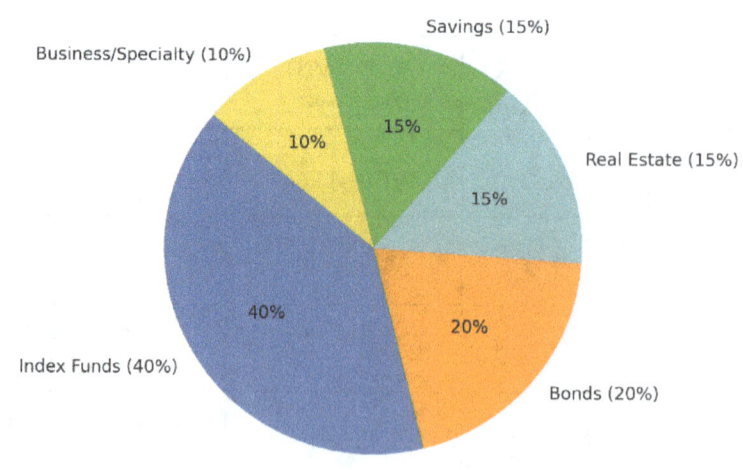

- **40% Index Funds** – Broad market exposure, long-term growth potential.

- **20% Bonds** – Lower risk, steady income, stability.

- **15% Real Estate** – Inflation hedge, tangible asset, potential rental income.

- **15% Savings** – Emergency fund, liquidity, security.

- **10% Business / Specialty Investments** – Higher risk, potential higher reward.

Reflection Questions

- What kind of investor are you: fearful, passive, or confident?
- What values guide your financial decisions?
- Have you asked God to direct your investments?

Encouragement You don't need thousands of dollars to begin. What you need is a faithful heart, a willing spirit, and a commitment to honor God with the growth He brings. Let your investments tell a story—not just of gain, but of grace.

Next Chapter Preview: Financial Challenges Facing Immigrants

Explore common obstacles like credit issues, family obligations, and financial isolation—and learn how to overcome them with wisdom and community.

Small, faithful steps
yield long-term fruit.

NOTES

Chapter 8

Unique Financial Challenges for Immigrants

Immigrants bring resilience, creativity, and an incredible work ethic. Yet they also face unique financial hurdles that can hinder their ability to thrive in the U.S. economy. Understanding these challenges is the first step to overcoming them. One of the most pressing challenges immigrants faces when entering the U.S. financial system is understanding and navigating how credit works and its impact. Because credit records from abroad generally do not transfer, one must build their financial reputation from scratch. This gap creates a cascade of hardships that touch nearly every aspect of daily life and has the ability to impact quality of life for future generations.

Without what is considered a good U.S. credit history, even the most responsible and financially disciplined individuals may be treated as high-risk. Many encounter obstacles renting housing without paying steep deposits, while others struggle to establish basic services like electricity, gas, or phone service. The absence of or poor credit can also drive-up costs: loans that would normally carry competitive rates may only be available at subprime levels, saddling families with high interest on car notes or personal credit. Some immigrants turn to costly alternatives such as money orders or check-cashing services, which may meet short-term needs but leave no pathway toward long-term financial stability.

This lack of access highlights a deeper problem: the tension between survival and stewardship. For immigrants who already carry the responsibility of supporting loved ones both in the U.S. and abroad, the added weight of being *"invisible"* to the financial system can feel overwhelming. Yet with intentional steps—such as opening a checking account, responsibly using secured or unsecured credit cards, and leaning into trusted financial education resources—immigrants can begin laying a new foundation. By understanding these barriers, readers can walk in wisdom, avoid traps that hinder progress, and move toward financial practices that honor God and build lasting stability.

1. Credit Invisibility
In the U.S., credit history is essential for securing housing, purchasing a car, or even getting a job. But many immigrants arrive with no credit file, making

them *"credit invisible."* This means:

- Higher interest rates or denied loans
- Difficulty renting homes
- Limited access to financial products

Biblical Insight: Proverbs 22:1 says, *"A good name is more desirable than great riches."*

> *In today's world, your 'good name' includes your credit score!*

Solutions:
- Apply for a secured credit card to begin building credit
- Become an authorized user on a trusted friend or family member's account
- Use rent or utility payments with services like Experian Boost

2. Remittance Responsibilities

Sending money home to family is an honorable and loving act. Yet it can put pressure on household finances.

- Some immigrants send up to 30% of their income back home
- Cultural and familial expectations can create guilt or conflict

Reflection: Ask, *"Am I giving beyond my means?"* God calls us to generosity, but not to self-neglect. Like the Good Samaritan, we must help from a place of capacity—not burnout.

Tips for Healthy Remittances:
- Set a monthly remittance budget
- Discuss boundaries with extended family
- Prioritize emergency funds and retirement savings

3. Cultural Norms and Mistrust of Formal Systems

Many come from regions where banks are unstable, exploitative, or corrupt. This leads to:

- Reluctance to open bank accounts
- Fear of debt or government programs
- Preference for cash transactions or informal saving circles

Steps Toward Confidence:
- Choose community-friendly banks or credit unions
- Attend financial literacy classes at churches or nonprofits
- Learn about consumer protections in the U.S.

4. Language Barriers and Information Gaps

Financial jargon is hard enough in English. For non-native speakers, it becomes overwhelming.

Support Systems:

- Look for programs offering bilingual financial coaching
- Use trusted resources like:
  - Amazon Community Lending Program (for small business support)
  - Local nonprofits such as immigrant advocacy centers

Effective Literacy Programs and Partnerships

Several organizations have created transformative programs.

Partnering with these groups can bridge the gap between biblical truth and financial literacy.

Worksheet: Barrier Identification and Action Plan

Barrier	Impact on My Finances	My Next Step
No credit history	Can't qualify for car loan	Apply for secured credit card
Family asks for remittances	Budget stress	Set monthly limit + communicate

Fear of banks	No savings account	Visit local credit union
Limited English	Avoid learning opportunities	Use translated resources

Encouragement: These challenges are real, but so is God's provision. Through prayer, wise counsel, and community support, you can turn obstacles into opportunities. The path to financial strength is not easy, but it is possible—and you don't have to walk it alone. Seek counsel.

Next Chapter Preview: Building a God-Honoring Financial Plan

How can you take everything you've learned and turn it into a holistic, biblically faithful financial strategy? Chapter 9 shows you how.

NOTES

Building a God-Honoring Financial Plan

Once you've learned the fundamentals—budgeting, saving, insurance, investing, and overcoming challenges—it's time to bring everything together into a financial plan that honors God and supports your future. This chapter guides you through creating a holistic plan based on biblical principles, personal vision, and intentional goal setting.

Why You Need a Financial Plan

A financial plan is a roadmap. Without one, it's easy to drift through life reacting to financial emergencies instead of preparing for them. A God-honoring plan is proactive, prayerful, and purposeful.

Biblical Foundation: Habakkuk 2:2

"Then the Lord replied: 'Write down the vision and make it plain on tablets so that a herald may run with it.'"

When we take time to write down our financial goals—anchored in biblical truth—we create clarity. We move from confusion to confidence, from fear to faith-filled action.

Step-by-Step: Creating a Vision-Based Financial Plan

Step 1: Pray for Direction Invite God into every part of your financial life. Ask for clarity, humility, and discernment.

"Commit to the Lord whatever you do, and He will establish your plans." – Proverbs 16:3

Step 2: Define Your Vision
- Where do you see yourself in 5, 10, 20 years?
- What kind of legacy do you want to leave?
- What does financial freedom look like to you?

Break this down into categories:

- **Spiritual Goals** (e.g., increase giving, fund a ministry)
- **Family Goals** (e.g., buy a home, fund college)
- **Career Goals** (e.g., start a business, get a degree)
- **Philanthropic Goals** (e.g., support family abroad, sponsor a child)

Step 3: Write SMART Goals

Make them:

- **Specific** – "Save $5,000 for emergency fund."
- **Measurable** – "Track savings each month."
- **Achievable** – "Cut dining out by $100 monthly."
- **Relevant** – "Build security for my family."
- **Time-bound** – "Reach goal within 12 months."

Step 4: Create a Budget That Reflects Your Vision

- Tithes and offerings
- Debt repayment
- Savings and investing
- Needs vs. wants

Step 5: Establish an Emergency Fund

- Start with $500 with an aim to get to $1000, then grow to 3–6 months of expenses.

Start Small, Grow Big

- Even $10 a week = $520 a year.
- Add $10 more monthly = $120 extra.
- Over 10 years, that's $6,400 plus remember interest to be added!
  ☐ "Whoever gathers money little by little makes it grow." (Proverbs 13:11)

Step 6: Plan Long-Term Milestones

- College funding
- Retirement
- Home ownership
- Giving goals

Step 7: Review and Revise Quarterly Financial plans must evolve with your life changes. Set a reminder every 3 months to reflect and adjust.

Step 8: Join an Accountability Group Surround yourself with others who also seek to honor God financially. Whether it's a small group at church or a trusted mentor, accountability helps you stay on track.

Suggestions:

- Host a monthly check-in
- Share prayer requests and victories
- Read a stewardship book together

Practical Tip: Look for programs or churches that offer financial literacy classes tailored to immigrant communities.

Worksheet: Vision Board Template

Instructions: Cut out or draw pictures, quotes, or scriptures that reflect your financial goals and values in the sections below. Use this board to inspire and revisit your plan.

Area of Life	Words/Images/Verses
Spiritual	e.g., Malachi 3:10, generosity, mission giving
Family	e.g., family home, kids' college, travel
Career	e.g., graduation, promotion, business growth
Philanthropy	e.g., donation box, community center
Retirement	e.g., peaceful living, security, gardening

Reflection Questions

- What fears are holding you back from planning?
- What does success look like through God's eyes?
- Who will hold you accountable to stay on this path?

Encouragement Jeremiah 29:11 reminds us that God has plans to prosper us—not to harm us. A God-honoring financial plan is more than dollars and cents—it's about trusting the One who holds your future.

Next Chapter Preview: Final Words of Encouragement

Because we can do all things through Christ who strengthens us…. go forth and share your story!

NOTES

10 Immediate Financial Steps to take

"Commit to the Lord whatever you do, and he will establish your plans." (Proverbs 16:3)

Step
1. Open a checking and savings account – Build a safe place to manage and grow your money.
2. Track every expense for 30 days – Awareness is the first step to financial control.
3. Build an emergency fund (start with $500) – A small cushion prevents small problems from becoming crises.
4. Learn how your credit score works – Good credit opens doors; poor credit closes them.
5. Avoid predatory loans or quick-cash traps – Don't sacrifice long-term peace for short-term fixes.
6. Get basic health and life insurance – Protect yourself and your family from unexpected costs.
7. File taxes on time and correctly – Stay compliant and possibly qualify for refunds or credits.
8. Start giving/tithing consistently – Honor God and cultivate generosity.
9. Set up a retirement savings account (401k/IRA) – Even small contributions today grow over time.
10. Teach your children basic money principles – Pass on wisdom and stewardship to the next generation.

NOTES

Chapter 10

Final Words of Encouragement

Dear Reader,

If you've made it this far, you've journeyed through truth, challenge, and hope. And I want to tell you, from the bottom of my heart: you are not alone, and your financial story is not finished.

Many immigrants feel overwhelmed, unseen, or discouraged when navigating the financial systems of a new land. But God's promises extend across every culture, economy, and border. His Word is timeless, and His provision is limitless.

Proverbs 15:22 tells us, *"Plans fail for lack of counsel, but with many advisers they succeed."* As immigrants navigating a new financial system, it's easy to feel overwhelmed. God never intended for us to walk this journey alone. The Bible reminds us that wise counsel brings success. This applies to finances as much as any other area of life.

Practical Application:

- **Talk to a trusted financial advisor or mentor** who understands both the U.S. system and your cultural background.

- **Seek advice from your church community** — many congregations have professionals willing to guide others.

- **Don't make major financial decisions alone** (like buying a house, taking a loan, or investing). Pause, pray, and get wise input first.

Seeking godly counsel doesn't make you weak — it makes you strong, because you're standing on wisdom, not just your own understanding.

Proverbs 16:3 says, *"Commit to the Lord whatever you do, and He will establish your plans."* You may not know every step ahead—but God does. When you surrender your financial goals to Him, He will shape them, sanctify them, and supply what you need to walk them out.

Luke 16:11 reminds us, *"So if you have not been trustworthy in handling worldly wealth, who will trust you with true riches?"* Financial stewardship is not just a practical responsibility—it's a spiritual calling. It is how we demonstrate faithfulness in the small things, so we can be entrusted with more.

Philippians 4:19 is your anchor: *"And my God will meet all your needs according to the riches of his glory in Christ Jesus."*

No matter your income, credit score, or mistakes of the past—God is faithful. You can make new decisions. You can change your family's legacy. You can use the 90% just as worshipfully as the tithe. It is all His, and He delights in seeing His children walk in wisdom and freedom.

Let this book not be a final word, but a beginning—a launching pad for a transformed life.

Spiritual Applications for Ongoing Stewardship

1. **Daily Prayer for Wisdom** – Ask God each morning to guide your spending and financial decisions.
2. **Scripture Memorization** – Write verses on your fridge or wallet to remind you of God's truth.
3. **Family Conversations** – Teach your children about stewardship early. Involve your spouse in financial prayer and planning.
4. **Community Support** – Join or start a small group focused on biblical finances.
5. **Regular Giving** – Even in scarcity, prioritize generosity. It keeps your heart anchored in God's abundance.

Legacy Building Steps
1. Write a will/create a Trust
2. Open a custodial savings account for children.
3. Teach tithing & generosity at home.
4. Model wise stewardship.

You are now equipped to honor God with every dollar—not just the tithe, but the other 90%.

Walk forward in confidence, beloved steward. The journey continues—and He walks with you.

You can honor God with your finances, no matter your income, background, or past mistakes. Faithfulness is the key.

*Key Verse: Proverbs 16:3 - *"Commit to the Lord whatever you do, and he will establish your plans."*

Closing Prayer

Father God, Thank You for the reader of this book. For the courage they've shown in facing their finances. For the hope that now stirs within them. Lord, establish the work of their hands. Multiply their efforts. Guard their hearts from fear. May they be stewards who reflect Your heart—generous, wise, and faithful. Let their lives testify that You are Jehovah Jireh, the God who provides. In Jesus' name, Amen.

Recommended Resources for Further Study

Books:

- *Financial Stewardship Bible* – Bibles.com / American Bible Society

About the Author

Valencia Maponya, MBA, is a passionate advocate for financial literacy, faith-based stewardship, and immigrant empowerment. As an immigrant herself, Valencia understands firsthand the challenges and opportunities that come with navigating a new financial system. Her deep-rooted passion for finances and human wellness stems from a lifelong belief that financial health is inextricably linked to overall well-being.

Despite being educated, Valencia has faced her seasons of personal financial struggle. These experiences have deepened her empathy and strengthened her conviction that God desires His children to live in financial freedom. Valencia is particularly encouraged by the potential within immigrant communities and believes that equipping them with financial literacy can lead to transformational change.

With over three decades of experience working alongside Caribbean, African, and Latin American immigrant populations, whether in healthcare, education or finance. Valencia has led financial education workshops, community development programs, and ministry initiatives that help families break the cycle of poverty and live with purpose. She believes that teaching financial principles to the younger generation is essential for generational change.

Blending biblical wisdom with practical tools, Valencia specializes in helping individuals and families steward their resources in ways that honor God and transform legacies. As a ministry leader and former financial advisor, she brings a compassionate, culturally aware approach to teaching financial principles.

Whether in a church hall, a city classroom, or across digital platforms, Valencia believes every person—regardless of background—can learn to manage money with wisdom, generosity, and joy. This book, *What About the Other 90%?* is part of that mission: to equip immigrant families with faith-filled guidance for financial freedom and legacy-building.

Appendix

Resources for Immigrants

These resources are researched and provided as tools to the reader. The author is not paid by any of the entities and should not be construed as endorsement.

🧾 Tax Preparation

» IRS Volunteer Income Tax Assistance (VITA): Free tax help for people who qualify (often immigrants, those with limited English, or lower-income households).

» 👉 https://www.irs.gov/individuals/free-tax-return-preparation-for-qualifying-taxpayers

» ITIN Application (Form W-7): For immigrants without a Social Security Number who still need to file taxes.

» 👉 https://www.irs.gov/individuals/individual-taxpayer-identification-number

»

🏢 Banking & Credit

» FDIC Bank Locator: Find insured banks you can trust. 👉 https://banks.data.fdic.gov/bankfind-suite/bankfind

» AnnualCreditReport.com: The only free, federally authorized site to check your credit report from Equifax, Experian, and TransUnion. 👉 https://www.

annualcreditreport.com

» National Credit Union Locator: Many credit unions are immigrant-friendly and offer fairer fees. 👉 https://mapping.ncua.gov

🪙 Budgeting & Saving Tools

» Mint (free app): Helps you track spending and create a budget. 👉 https://mint.intuit.com

» EveryDollar (Dave Ramsey): A Christian-based budgeting app that aligns with stewardship principles. 👉 https://www.everydollar.com

» YNAB (You Need A Budget): Paid app with powerful planning tools. 👉 https://www.ynab.com

🛡 Insurance & Protection

» National Association of Insurance Commissioners (NAIC): Guides for life insurance, health insurance, and avoiding scams. 👉 https://content.naic.org/consumer

🏦 Health Insurance for Immigrants

» Healthcare.gov (Affordable Care Act Marketplace): Official U.S. site to apply for health insurance, compare plans, and see if you qualify for subsidies. Many lawfully present immigrants are eligible. 👉 https://www.healthcare.gov

» State Health Marketplaces: Some states (like California, New York, and Massachusetts) offer additional coverage options for immigrants. 👉 https://www.healthcare.gov/marketplace-in-your-state

» Medicaid & CHIP: Low-cost or free health insurance for

eligible low-income families and children, depending on immigration status and state. 👉 https://www.medicaid.gov

» Community Health Centers: Regardless of immigration status, federally funded clinics provide affordable primary care. 👉 https://findahealthcenter.hrsa.gov

📚 Financial Literacy & Immigrant Resources

» MyMoney.gov (U.S. Treasury): Free financial education materials. 👉 https://www.mymoney.gov

» Consumer Financial Protection Bureau (CFPB): Immigrant-friendly guides on banking, credit, and avoiding predatory loans. 👉 https://www.consumerfinance.gov

» Immigrant Finance Project: Community platform helping immigrants learn about investing, banking, and entrepreneurship. 👉 https://immigrantfinance.com

🌍 Remittances & Global Support

» World Bank Remittance Prices: Compare costs of sending money home and find safer, cheaper options. 👉 https://remittanceprices.worldbank.org

» Wise (formerly TransferWise): Low-cost, transparent money transfer service. 👉 https://wise.com

🙏 Faith & Stewardship Ministries

» Crown Financial Ministries: Biblical resources for financial stewardship. 👉 https://www.crown.org

» Compass – Finances God's Way: Small-group studies and practical tools for applying Scripture to money. 👉

👉 https://compass1.org

✨ Tip: Identify two or three of these resources and begin using them right away. Small, consistent steps can reshape your financial journey for generations.

www.ingramcontent.com/pod-product-compliance
Lightning Source LLC
Chambersburg PA
CBHW070447130626
46553CB00006B/2302